A glass timeline

75,000 BCE

People use natural glass to make arrowheads, knives and other sharp blades.

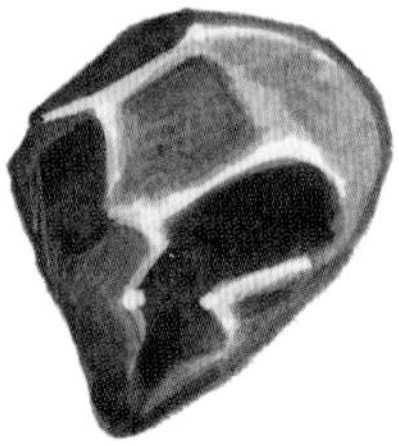

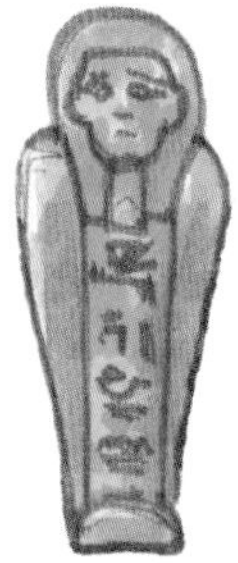

1,500 BCE

The Egyptians make small glass jars, vases and jewellery.

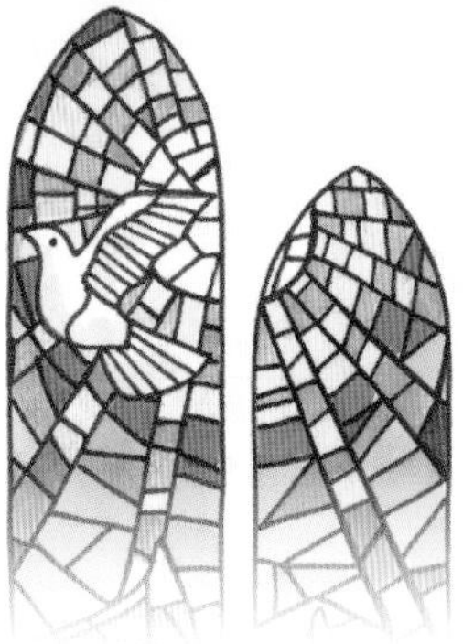

7th century

Stained glass windows begin to appear in churches and monasteries.

3,500 BCE

People in Egypt and Mesopotamia (Iraq today) discover how to make glass.

1st century CE

Glassblowing makes bowls, vases and other hollow glass objects easier, cheaper and faster to produce. The Romans take glass with them all over their growing empire.

1870s

The first bottle-making machines are built, making it possible to manufacture bottles in large numbers very quickly.

1608

Glassmaking begins in America, and glass windows become more common in Europe, even among poor people.

1959

The float glass process is introduced in Britain by Alastair Pilkington, enabling glassmakers to manufacture very smooth, flat glass more cheaply.

1674

Lead glass is invented in Britain by George Ravenscroft. Adding lead to glass improved its appearance and made it easier for glassmakers to melt and work with.

2000

Self-cleaning glass is invented in Britain. A thin chemical coating on the glass helps to break down dirt so that rain can wash it away.

1890s

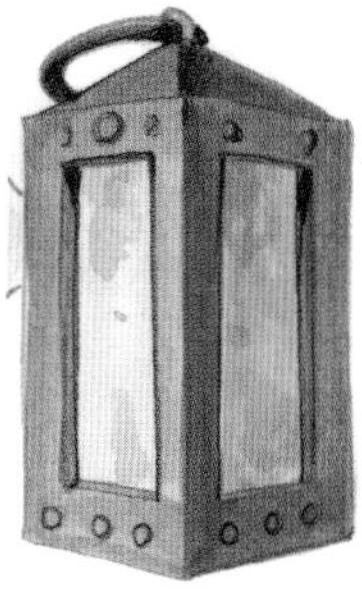

German chemist Otto Schott invents borosilicate glass, a type of glass that can withstand sudden temperature changes. It is used to make glass saucepans and ovenproof dishes.

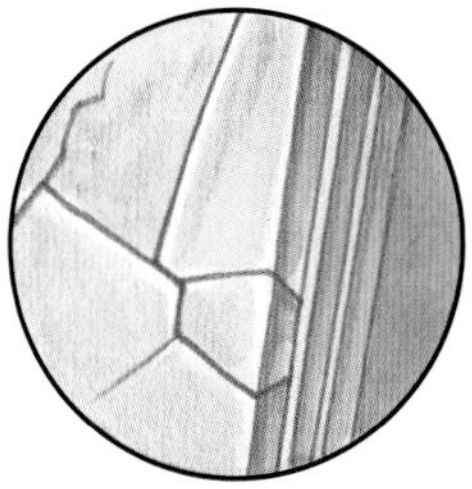

What is glass?

Glass is a solid material. It is made of particles called atoms. The atoms in most solid materials are linked together in a neat pattern that repeats itself again and again. If you could see the atoms in a grain of sand, you would see them lined up in identical groups forming this regular, repeating pattern. Glass is made from sand, but the atoms in glass are linked together differently from sand.

Glass is made by heating sand until it melts. When sand melts, the links between some of its atoms break and so the atoms are able to move around. When the liquid sand cools down and begins to set hard, the atoms form new links with each other. Instead of the neat, regular crystal structure of sand, the atoms in glass are linked together in a messy, random way.

Author:
Ian Graham earned a degree in applied physics at City University, London. He then took a graduate diploma in journalism. Since becoming a freelance author and journalist, he has written more than 250 children's nonfiction books.

Artist:
Mark Bergin was born in Hastings, England, in 1961. He studied at Eastbourne College of Art and specialises in historical reconstructions, aviation and maritime subjects. He lives in Bexhill-on-Sea with his wife and children.

Series creator:
David Salariya was born in Dundee, Scotland. He has illustrated a wide range of books and has created and designed many new series for publishers in the UK and overseas. David established The Salariya Book Company in 1989. He lives in Brighton with his wife, illustrator Shirley Willis, and their son Jonathan.

Editor: Jacqueline Ford

Editorial Assistant: Mark Williams

PAPER FROM
SUSTAINABLE
FORESTS

Published in Great Britain in MMXVII by
Book House, an imprint of
The Salariya Book Company Ltd
25 Marlborough Place, Brighton BN1 1UB
www.salariya.com
www.book-house.co.uk

ISBN: 978-1-911242-28-4

SALARIYA

1 3 5 7 9 8 6 4 2

A CIP catalogue record for this book is available from the British Library.

Printed and bound in China.

You Wouldn't Want to Live Without™

Glass!

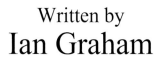

Written by
Ian Graham

Illustrated by
Mark Bergin

Series created by
David Salariya

BOOK HOUSE
a SALARIYA imprint

Contents

Introduction

You use glass from morning till night every day, from the mirror you look in when you wash your face in the morning to the lightbulbs that brighten your home after dark. All sorts of foods and drinks are stored in glass bottles and jars, and many of your electronic gadgets have glass screens. Cameras and binoculars have lenses made of glass. The signals that carry your phone calls and texts – and websites when you're online – make part of their journey along glass communications cables. Every home, school and workplace has glass windows. Can you imagine what your world and your life would be like if there were no glass? Buildings would have no windows. There would be no lenses for cameras or microscopes. There would probably be no televisions or computers. You really wouldn't want to live without glass.

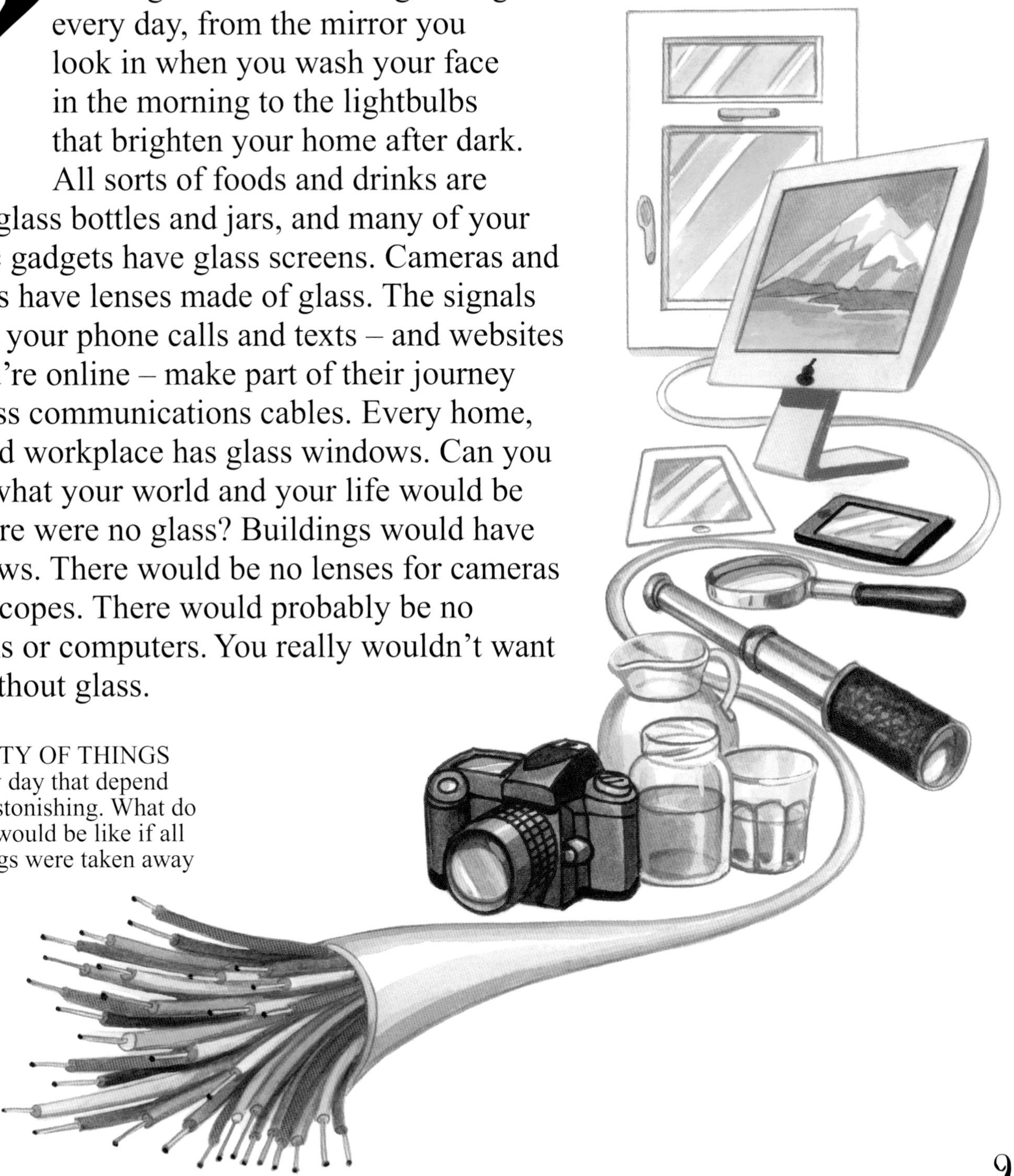

THE VARIETY OF THINGS we use every day that depend on glass is astonishing. What do you think it would be like if all of these things were taken away from you?

What if there were no glass?

If people had never discovered how to make glass, many of the things you use would be different, and some might never have been invented at all. For example, polished metal might make a good mirror…until it gets scratched and dented. Nowadays, we could use clear plastic to replace glass, but if glass windows, screens and bottles had never existed, would anyone have thought of the idea of inventing clear plastic?

LOOK AROUND YOU and see how many things you can spot that have glass parts. Are you wearing a watch or about to grab a glass of water? Is it time for your favourite programme on TV? Glass is just about everywhere!

You can do it!

If there were no glass for mirrors, what else could you make a mirror from? Try kitchen foil, polished metal and anything else you can think of. Do any of them work?

DARK CITIES. Cities all over the world are flooded with light at night. It shines out through glass windows and from glass street lamps. Shopfronts are lit up by neon signs too. Without glass for windows, lights and glowing signs, our cities would be much darker places.

TRAFFIC CHAOS? Traffic at busy road junctions is often controlled by coloured light signals. They keep the traffic moving and stop the junction from being blocked. If there were no glass, traffic lights might never have been invented and traffic jams, or gridlock, might be a lot more common today.

Nature's glass

All the glass you see and use every day is manufactured. It was made by someone or by a machine. It is the size, shape and colour it is because it was designed and made like that. But even if people had never discovered how to make glass, we would still know about glass because it is also made in nature. In fact, nature has been making glass on Earth for billions of years. Any event in nature that produces enough heat to melt rock or sand is capable of making glass. Natural glass is produced by volcanoes and lightning, and also when large meteorites hit the ground. Meteorites are chunks of rock from space that survive their fiery journey down through Earth's atmosphere and land on the ground.

What's this?
It's volcanic glass.

VOLCANIC GLASS. When lava (hot liquid rock) from a volcano cools slowly, it becomes rock. But if it cools quickly, there is not enough time for the microscopic crystals that form rock to grow. Instead of rock, the result is volcanic glass. One of the best-known types of volcanic glass is called obsidian. It's hard and brittle, and usually black.

LIGHTNING GLASS. When lightning strikes the ground, it instantly heats the spot to about 2,500ºC (4,500ºF). That's hot enough to melt sand and change it to glass. As a lightning bolt travels down into the ground, it forms long, branching tubes of glass up to 5 metres (17 feet) long. These antler-like pieces of glass created by lightning are called fulgurites.

How it works

Natural glass is rarely clear like a window, because it often includes small minerals that give it colour, has a rough, uneven surface, lots of tiny cracks, and partly melted rock or sand sticking to it.

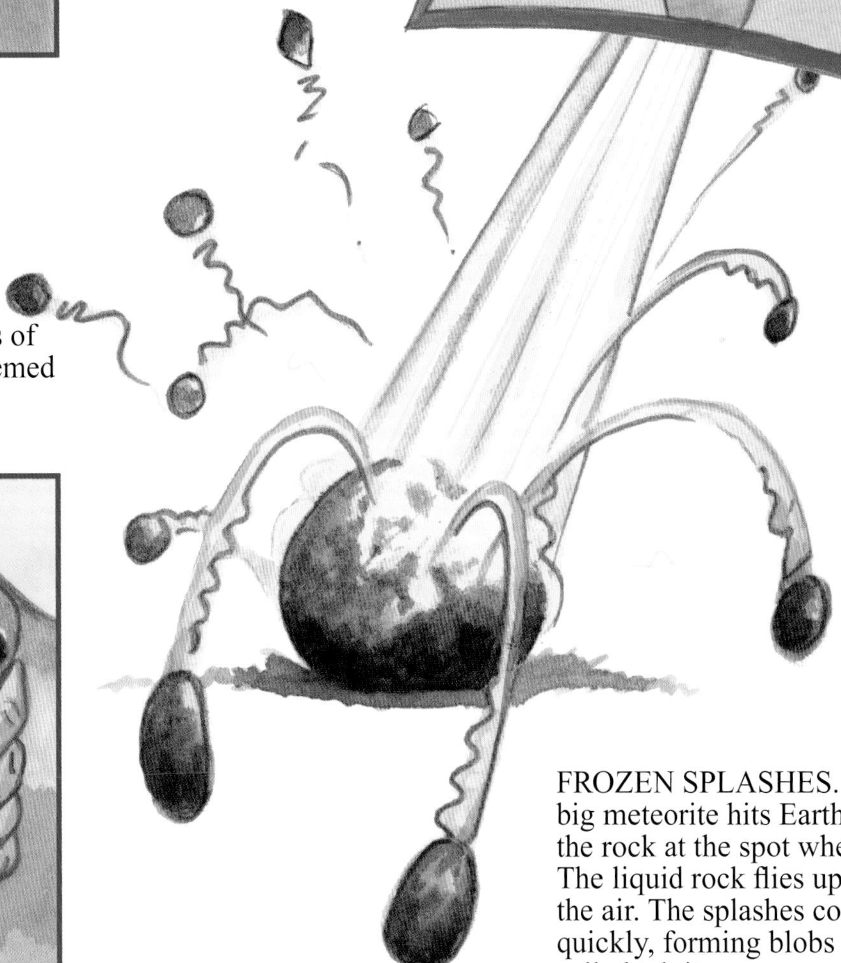

MYSTERY MATERIAL. Thousands of years ago, our distant ancestors found pieces of natural glass. It must have seemed magical to them, quite unlike anything else in nature.

FROZEN SPLASHES. When a big meteorite hits Earth, it melts the rock at the spot where it lands. The liquid rock flies up into the air. The splashes cool down quickly, forming blobs of glass called tektites.

Before we made glass

Imagine if you lived in Europe about 500 years ago. You probably wouldn't own anything made of glass unless you were very wealthy. The windows in your home wouldn't have any glass in them. You wouldn't have any drinking cups made of glass. Instead you would drink from pottery cups, or – if you're lucky – goblets made of gold, silver or a cheaper metal called pewter. You probably wouldn't even know what you look like, because you wouldn't own a glass mirror. You would have to get by without these things or use other materials instead of glass.

IF YOU HAD LIVED hundreds of years ago and you didn't have a mirror, the only time you might see your reflection would be when you spotted it in a pool of water. It might have been quite a surprise to see what you looked like!

I wish there were a bit more daylight...

Top tip

As a person living in Europe in the Middle Ages, you'll want to wrap up during the winter. Since glass windows haven't been invented yet, it can be pretty draughty indoors!

HORN AND HIDE. Until about 400 years ago, the windows in many people's homes were either open to the weather or covered with animal hide or pieces of animal horn. The horn was so thin that it let some light through. Horn was much cheaper than glass, which was heavily taxed in some countries.

17th-century candle lantern with sheets of mica

MICA. Thin sheets of a material called mica were used instead of glass in some windows and lanterns. Mica is a naturally occurring rock that can be split into very thin sheets. It was used, like animal horn, as a cheaper alternative to glass. It is also known as Muscovy glass.

BEFORE GLASS BOTTLES became widely available, bottles and other containers were made of clay pottery, metal or even leather. When clay bottles broke, they were thrown away. They were so common that archaeologists often find them buried in the ground.

A new material

People have been using glass for thousands of years. At first, it was glass they found in nature. They used it to make blades. The ancient Aztec people of Mexico made cutting tools and weapons from natural glass. They also made glass jewellery. About 5,500 years ago, people in Mesopotamia and Egypt discovered how to make glass. They made glassy glazes for their pottery and then small glass objects such as beads. Larger items came later as their skills improved. If they had not learned how to make glass, we might not have the glass things that are so useful to us today.

AN ANCIENT AZTEC SWORD called a macuahuitl is a fearsome weapon. It was used right up to the sixteenth century. A macuahuitl was made by setting slivers of black obsidian glass along the edges of a wooden sword. The result was a weapon up to 1.2 metres (4 feet) long and 8 cm (3 in) across, weighing a hefty 3 kg (6.6 lb). It was even sharper than a modern steel razor blade.

THE SECRET OF GLASSMAKING was probably discovered by accident. Perhaps some sand melted in a metalworking furnace and changed into glass. Maybe sand stuck to wet clay in a pottery kiln and formed a glassy glaze. It must have happened many times before anyone noticed, and many more times before someone thought of making glass deliberately by melting sand in a furnace.

How it works

Ancient glass beads usually have a hole in the middle, because they were strung together as a necklace or bracelet. The thread rotted away, but the glass beads can still be found today.

THE ANCIENT EGYPTIANS made a glassy substance called faience. They made it by grinding up sand with other materials to produce a crunchy, clay-like material. They then moulded this into the shape of jewellery or small figures, and heated it in a furnace. The mixture partly melted and hardened, forming a glassy surface.

THE ANCIENT ROMANS were expert glassmakers. About 2,000 years ago, they were making all sorts of glass cups, bowls and bottles. And they took their glassware with them all over the vast Roman Empire.

WHEN ARCHEOLOGISTS dig among ancient buildings or graves, they often find glass beads. They were worn as jewellery and traded for other items and services. They can help archaeologists to date a site. Finding the same type of beads in different places can also help to show which settlements were trading with each other.

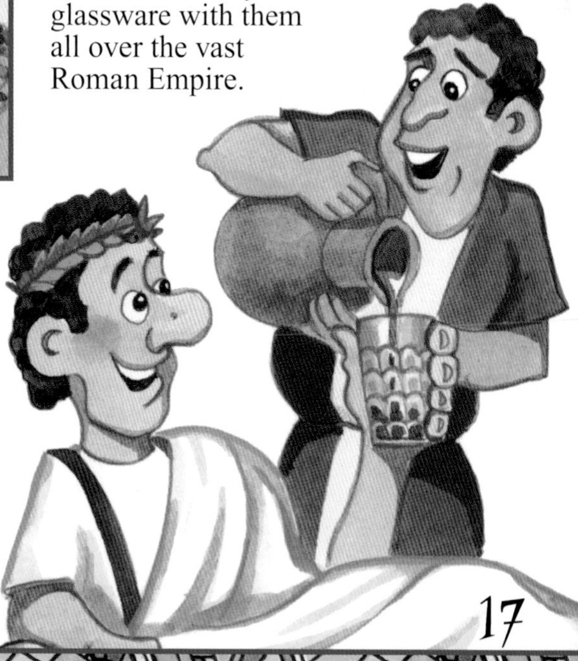

Making glass

People make glass in a way that is very similar to how nature does it. They heat sand until it melts. Other substances are often added to help the sand melt and to colour the glass. Adding small amounts of iron or chromium produces green glass. Cobalt and copper turn glass blue. Gold produces a red colour. Glass used to be coloured yellow by using radioactive uranium, until the dangers of uranium were discovered.

Once glass is made, it has to be shaped. Glass bottles, bowls and other items can be made one at a time by skilled people, or they can be made more quickly in large numbers by using special machines.

A GLASSBLOWER makes hollow items by blowing air through a pipe into a blob of molten glass on the end of the pipe. The glass, at a temperature of just over 1,000ºC (1,800ºF), looks like soft toffee and blows up like a balloon.

Furnace
Sand
Flux
Stabiliser

You can do it!
You can help to save materials and energy by recycling glass so that it can be used again. Old broken glass called cullet is added to new materials to make new glass.
RECYCLE

FOLLOW THE RECIPE. Glass is made of three basic materials: a former, a flux and a stabiliser. The most common type of glass is called soda-lime glass. The former, or main substance, is silica (sand). The flux, usually sodium oxide from soda, lowers the sand's melting temperature. The stabiliser, usually calcium oxide from limestone, stops the glass from dissolving or crumbling after it cools and hardens.

THE MACHINES THAT MAKE GLASS BOTTLES use a process called blow moulding. They lower a tube of glowing glass, called a gob, into a metal mould. The mould closes around the glass. Then air is blown in to inflate the glass and press it against the walls of the mould. This makes the glass take the shape of the mould. Finally, the mould opens and a glowing-hot glass bottle emerges.

Clearly useful

The most useful property of glass is its transparency – its ability to let light pass through. It lets you see what kind of solid or liquid – and how much – is inside bottles and jars. And this transparency allows light out of lightbulbs. The glass bulb also keeps air out. Without glass bulbs, electric lights would burn out in seconds. If there were no glass, we might have to go back to using candles and gas lamps for lighting. And of course TV sets, computers, mobile phones, wristwatches and other electronic gadgets would be useless without their glass screens.

BULLS-EYE WINDOWS. In the 1300s, French glassmakers invented a way to make glass for windows by spinning molten glass to make a flat disc. The middle was thicker than the edges. It was known as bulls-eye glass, or crown glass.

WITHOUT GLASS, you'd always have to open storage jars to find out what's inside.

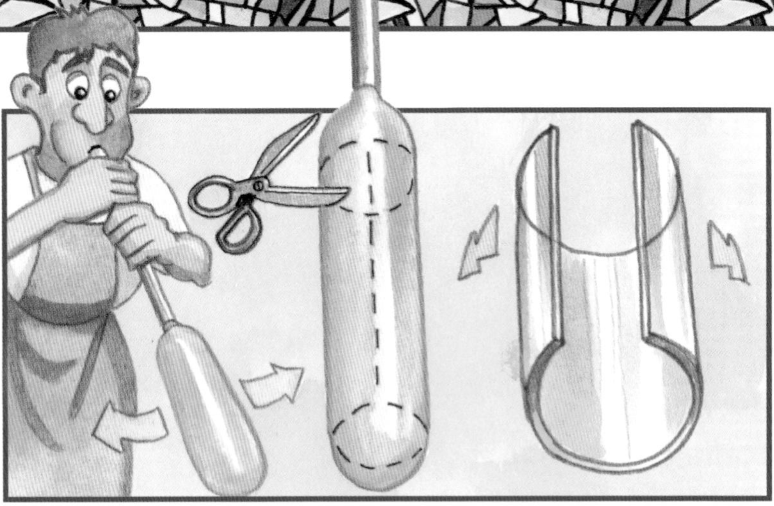

How it works

Greenhouses work by letting sunlight pass through their glass roof and walls to warm everything inside. Then the glass traps the warm air inside so that it can't be blown away.

THE CYLINDER METHOD. By the 1800s, windows were flatter than the old bulls-eye panes, because they were being made in a new way. They started as a long tube of glass, like a long party balloon. While the glass was still hot and soft, the ends were cut off and the cylinder was slit from end to end. The slit cylinder was then opened out to make a flat sheet.

FLOATING FLAT. Modern window glass is very flat because of the way it is made. Hot glass is laid on the surface of molten tin. As the glass cools, it forms a perfectly flat sheet called float glass.

LABORATORY GLASS. The test tubes and flasks used in science laboratories are made of glass so that scientists can see what is happening to the chemicals inside them. Also, the glass doesn't react with chemicals and change them in unwanted ways.

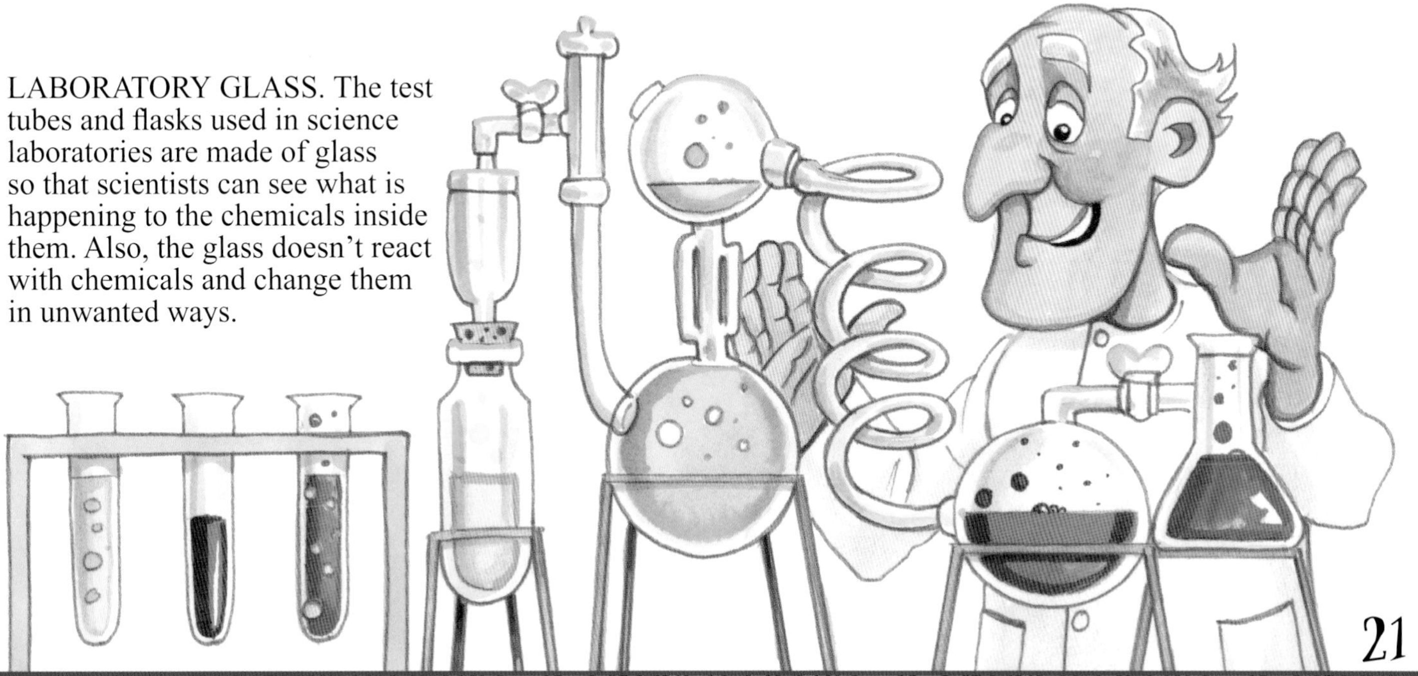

Making it safe

Imagine a train or a car with no glass in its windows. Would you like to go for a trip in it on a cold day or when it's raining? Glass windows make trains, cars and other vehicles weatherproof. In the past, vehicle windows were made of ordinary glass, but this proved to be dangerous. If a window broke it would send razor-sharp pieces of glass flying everywhere, so safer types of glass were invented. They still sometimes break, but they break in a safer way. Without them, travelling would be more dangerous.

A CAR WITHOUT GLASS would not be much fun to travel in. Luckily, glass was invented before cars. Today, car windows are made of two different types of safety glass – laminated glass and toughened glass. Toughened glass is toughened, or tempered, by treating it with heat or chemicals.

CRUMBS! When toughened glass breaks, it shatters into thousands of small glass crumbs. The rounded crumbs are less likely to cause injuries than the sharp splinters produced by ordinary glass. Toughened glass is used for a car's side windows and rear windows.

Top tip

Newspaper is very good for cleaning glass. Some people think the ink on the paper polishes the glass. Others think it works because the paper is very absorbent. What do you think?

A GLASS SANDWICH. A car's windshield is made of laminated glass. It's a sandwich of sheets of glass with plastic between them. Laminated glass is used in places where the glass must stay together even when it breaks, such as skyscraper windows.

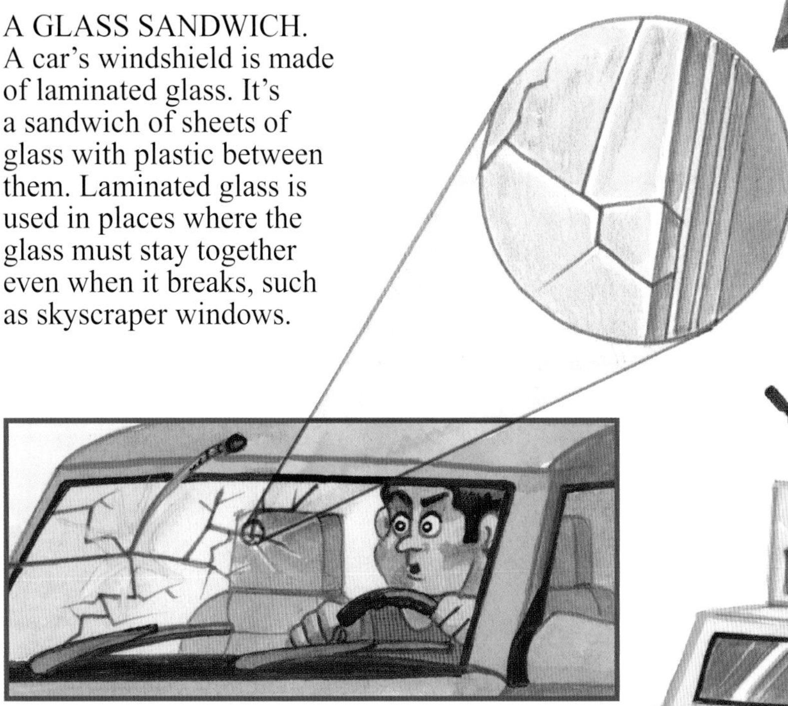

BULLETPROOF. A window made of several layers of thick glass and plastic up to about 9 cm (3.5 in) thick can stop a bullet. This type of bulletproof glass is used in places like banks, armoured cars and military vehicles.

STICKING TOGETHER. If a laminated windshield gets broken by a stone thrown up from the road, the glass might crack, but the plastic layer holds the pieces together and stops them from flying out and causing injuries.

Reflectors

The smooth, flat surface of a sheet of manufactured glass is very good at reflecting light. The reflection is brighter and clearer if the glass is coated with a thin film of shiny metal, forming a mirror. But mirrors do a lot more than let you check out your appearance. Without mirrors, we would know a lot less about the rest of the universe.

Astronomical telescopes use curved mirrors to focus light from distant stars and galaxies. The amazing photographs taken by the Hubble Space Telescope were made possible by the mirrors inside it. There are even mirrors on the moon. They were placed there by astronauts. Scientists use them to calculate the precise distance between Earth and the moon. Glass mirrors make driving safer, too.

THE HUBBLE SPACE TELESCOPE gathers light from distant parts of the universe. The light falls on a large primary mirror. It bounces onto a small secondary mirror and then into cameras and other instruments.

DRIVERS OFTEN NEED to know what's happening behind them. They do it by glancing in their rearview mirror. If there were no glass mirrors, drivers might have to take their eyes off the road and turn around, risking more accidents.

A REFLECTION in a mirror is accurate and lifelike only if the mirror is flat. Fairgrounds make use of this. Their distorting mirrors are curved and wavy. They make reflections of people look very odd. Some parts are bigger and others are smaller.

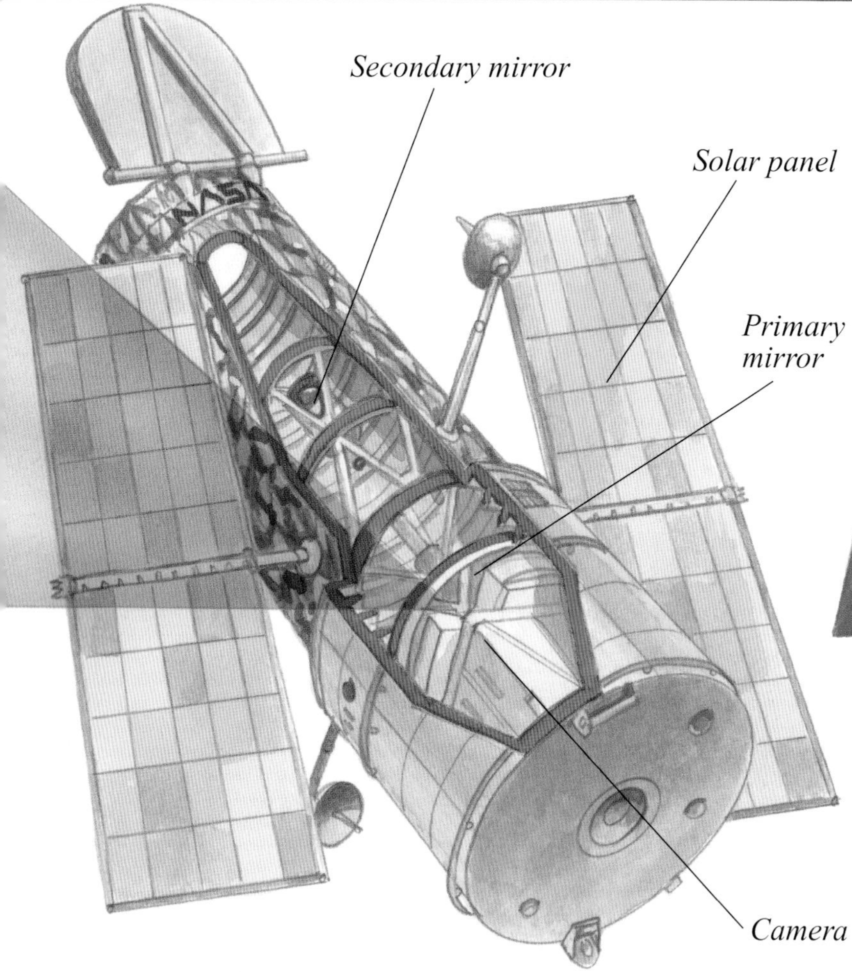

You can do it!

You can see the effect of a distorting mirror by looking at your reflection in the back of a spoon. Then turn the spoon over and see how different your reflection is in the other side.

THE GLASS STUDS that mark out roads at night work by reflecting light from a vehicle's headlights. They're called cat's eyes, because the inventor got the idea for them when he saw a real cat's eyes shining brightly in his car headlights one night.

A CURVED MIRROR can concentrate sunlight and produce very high temperatures. In 2013, the curved glass wall of a new building in London focused sunlight onto the street below. A car parked there partially melted! The building has a sunshade now.

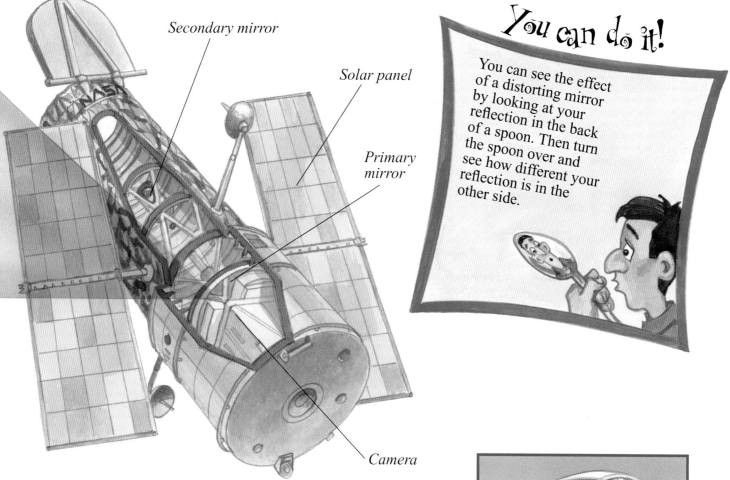

Light benders

Light slows down a little as it travels through glass. This has a strange effect on the light. As it hits the glass and slows down, it changes direction. It's an effect called refraction and it can be very useful. A piece of glass shaped in a special way can bend light rays together or spread them apart. A piece of glass that does this is called a lens. Bending light rays like this can make things look bigger or smaller, closer or further away. Because of this simple property of glass, we know more about everything from microscopic germs to vast galaxies of stars.

ONE OF THE FIRST THINGS astronomers used telescopes for was to look at the moon. They were amazed to see towering mountains, deep valleys, craters of all sizes and vast flat plains in wonderful close-up detail. Astronomers still use telescopes to study the moon today.

BEFORE GLASS LENSES became common, very few people had eyeglasses. Some of the monks who wrote manuscripts and read books were among the few to own a pair. The lenses were set in a frame made from bone, metal or leather that was balanced on the nose. Everyone else had to manage without glasses, no matter how poor their vision was.

You can do it!

You can see how glass bends light by putting a straw in a glass of water. The straw looks broken at the water's surface, because the light rays bend as they leave the glass of water.

SIR ISAAC NEWTON proved that sunlight contains light of all colours. He passed light through a glass wedge called a prism. The prism split the light into a rainbow of colours.

MICROSCOPES USE LENSES to magnify tiny things that are normally too small to be seen. The first microscopes in the 1590s revealed a hidden world of tiny organisms. Many of the organisms that cause diseases were discovered by scientists using microscopes.

Building with glass

You might think that glass is a very weak and fragile material. Windows and glass vases break easily, but glass in a different form is strong enough to use as a building material. And glass blocks are sturdy enough to be used for building walls. The front wall of a giant public aquarium is often made of extremely strong glass. Glass has other properties that are useful to the construction industry. In the form of glass wool, it traps air inside it, and air is a good insulator. Double-glazed windows use air as an insulator, too. Air trapped inside them reduces the amount of heat that passes through. Without glass wool insulation and double glazing, buildings would be colder in winter and hotter in summer.

THE GLASS WALL that forms the front of the world's biggest public aquariums can be up to 75 cm (30 in) thick. The glass has to be as thick as this to hold back the enormous weight of water behind it.

LARGE GLASS BLOCKS can be used like bricks to build walls and partitions inside buildings. They can be used outside in gardens too. A glass block wall can screen off a private space while letting light through.

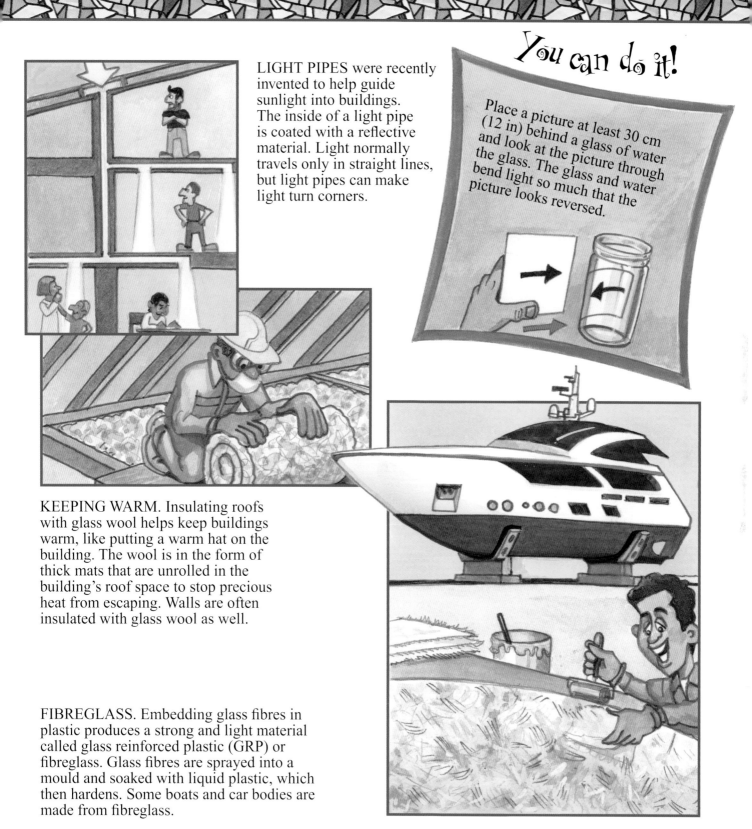

LIGHT PIPES were recently invented to help guide sunlight into buildings. The inside of a light pipe is coated with a reflective material. Light normally travels only in straight lines, but light pipes can make light turn corners.

You can do it!

Place a picture at least 30 cm (12 in) behind a glass of water and look at the picture through the glass. The glass and water bend light so much that the picture looks reversed.

KEEPING WARM. Insulating roofs with glass wool helps keep buildings warm, like putting a warm hat on the building. The wool is in the form of thick mats that are unrolled in the building's roof space to stop precious heat from escaping. Walls are often insulated with glass wool as well.

FIBREGLASS. Embedding glass fibres in plastic produces a strong and light material called glass reinforced plastic (GRP) or fibreglass. Glass fibres are sprayed into a mould and soaked with liquid plastic, which then hardens. Some boats and car bodies are made from fibreglass.

Glass art

Glass isn't used only to make practical everyday things like windows and television screens. It is also used by artists to make beautiful objects. Some artists specialise in making decorative glass vases, lampshades, jewellery and other items. Some of the biggest and most visually stunning works of art ever produced are made of glass. These include the stained-glass windows of the world's most famous churches and cathedrals. Without glass, there would be none of this wonderful art for us to enjoy.

STAINED GLASS WINDOWS in churches were designed to show events and tell stories to people who, in past centuries, could not read.

ÉMILE GALLÉ (1846–1904) was a French artist who made coloured glass vases and lampshades decorated with plants, insects and other natural objects.

How it works
Stained-glass windows are made by fitting pieces of coloured glass into lead channels and then joining the pieces of lead together by soldering (melting metal into the joints).

LOUIS COMFORT TIFFANY (1848–1933) was an American artist and designer famous for making stained glass objects including windows, jewellery and lamps.

RENÉ LALIQUE (1860–1945) was a French designer known for making beautiful glass vases, jewellery and ornaments. He also made glass screens and columns for decorating buildings and ocean liners.

The future of glass

Designers are thinking up exciting new uses for glass. Imagine living in a home with light-sensitive windows that darken automatically in bright sunshine. If you had windows that you could darken at night, you wouldn't need curtains. Bright sunshine can be a problem for drivers. Car windows that darken automatically would ease this problem. Imagine a skyscraper with glass walls that are also giant video screens. The wonderful things we continue to learn to do with glass make us realise how much we wouldn't want to live without it!

NEW TYPES OF GLASS and glass coatings are being developed for electronic products. Screens for mobile phones, tablets and other devices made from this glass will be easier to use in bright light.

MIRROR MIRROR. Scientists are developing a special kind of mirror that can assess the health of anyone who stands in front of it.

How it works

Vitrification changes radioactive waste into blocks of glass, stopping it from escaping into the environment. Processes like these will help to keep our planet clean in the future.

IN THE FUTURE, glass may become an increasingly popular packaging material once again because it does not taint, contaminate or react with its contents, and it is also totally recyclable.

SMART DESK. Using glass and technology, designers are developing exciting new ways to work and study. In the future, your desk might have a glass top that is also a touch-sensitive computer screen.

Glossary

Archeologist A scientist who studies human history, especially by digging up and examining the remains of people and their activities.

Astronomer A scientist who studies the stars, galaxies, planets, moons and other bodies in the universe.

Atmosphere The gases that surround Earth and some other bodies.

Crystal Any solid material made of particles (atoms or molecules) arranged in a regular, repeating pattern.

Double glazing The process of creating a window from two sheets of glass with a small gap between them.

Flux A substance that lowers the melting point of sand, which helps make it easier to produce glass.

Former The main substance used in making or 'forming' glass (usually silica, or sand).

Galaxy Millions or billions of stars travelling through space together, with giant clouds of gas and dust. We live in a galaxy called the Milky Way.

Germ A microscopic organism, especially one that causes disease.

Hide The skin of an animal.

Hubble Space Telescope An instrument in space that has been used by astronomers to study distant parts of the universe since 1990.

Insulation A material that stops or slows the spread of heat, sound or electricity.

Laminated glass A type of safety glass that holds together even if the glass breaks.

Lava Liquid rock that erupts from volcanoes, and the same rock when cool and hard.

Lens A piece of glass or another transparent material shaped so that it forms an image by bending light rays.

Meteorite A piece of rock or natural metal that has fallen to Earth from space and survived its impact with the ground.

Middle Ages The name given to the period of history between the fifth and fifteenth centuries.

Molten Made liquid by being heated to a very high temperature.

Organism A living plant or animal.

Primary mirror The main or biggest reflecting surface in an optical instrument such as a telescope.

Prism A piece of glass or other transparent material, often triangular in shape, used for separating white light into the colours of which it is made up.

Radioactive Giving out particles or rays by a process called radioactive decay.

Roman Empire A group of nations and tribes, mainly around the Mediterranean Sea, that were conquered and then governed by the ancient Romans.

Secondary mirror The second, or smaller, reflecting surface inside an optical instrument such as a telescope. It reflects light from the larger primary mirror.

Stabiliser A substance that stops glass from dissolving or crumbling once it cools and hardens.

Tektite A small black piece of glass formed when a meteorite hits the ground and sends out splashes of molten rock. Each splash cools down to form a tektite.

Toughened glass A type of safety glass that forms small rounded crumbs of glass instead of sharp splinters when it breaks. Also called tempered glass.

Vitrification The process of changing a substance into glass by heating it to a very high temperature with glass-forming materials.

Index

Top glassmakers

George Ravenscroft (1632–1683)
Ravenscroft learned about glassmaking while working in Venice. In 1666 he returned to England and started his own glassmaking business. The glass being made in England at that time would become cloudy and cracked after a year or two, a problem called crizzling. Ravenscroft experimented with different materials. He discovered that adding lead oxide improved the glass. What became known as lead glass was a sparkling, hard glass that lasted longer and didn't suffer from crizzling.

Joseph Paxton (1803–1865)
Paxton was an English gardener who worked for the Duke of Devonshire. He built an iron and glass conservatory at the duke's stately home, Chatsworth. When he heard that all the designs for a building to house the Great Exhibition in London had been rejected, he sent his own design based on his conservatory. It was accepted, because it was inexpensive and quick and easy to build. The building became famous as the Crystal Palace. Paxton received a knighthood for his work, which marked the beginning of glass as a building material.

Sir Alastair Pilkington (1920–1995)
After studying mechanical engineering at Cambridge University, Pilkington went to work for the Pilkington glass company. (He had no connection with the Pilkington family who founded the company, it was just a funny coincidence.) While working there he came up with the idea of making flat glass by floating it on molten tin. He perfected the method in 1959, making it possible to produce high-quality flat glass without having to grind and polish it.

Prince Rupert's Drop

When a blob of molten glass is dropped into cold water, it quickly cools and sets hard, forming a glass droplet with a long, thin tail. It looks a little like a glass tadpole. A piece of glass like this is called a Prince Rupert's Drop, and it behaves in a very strange way.

The head of a Prince Rupert's Drop is surprisingly strong. In fact, you can even hit it with a hammer and it won't break. However, the tail of a Prince Rupert's Drop is very different from the head. If the thin tail is broken, the whole thing explodes! This is because the glass on the outside of a Prince Rupert's Drop cools faster than the glass on the inside. This produces enormous forces, which make the glass explode spectacularly when it is broken.

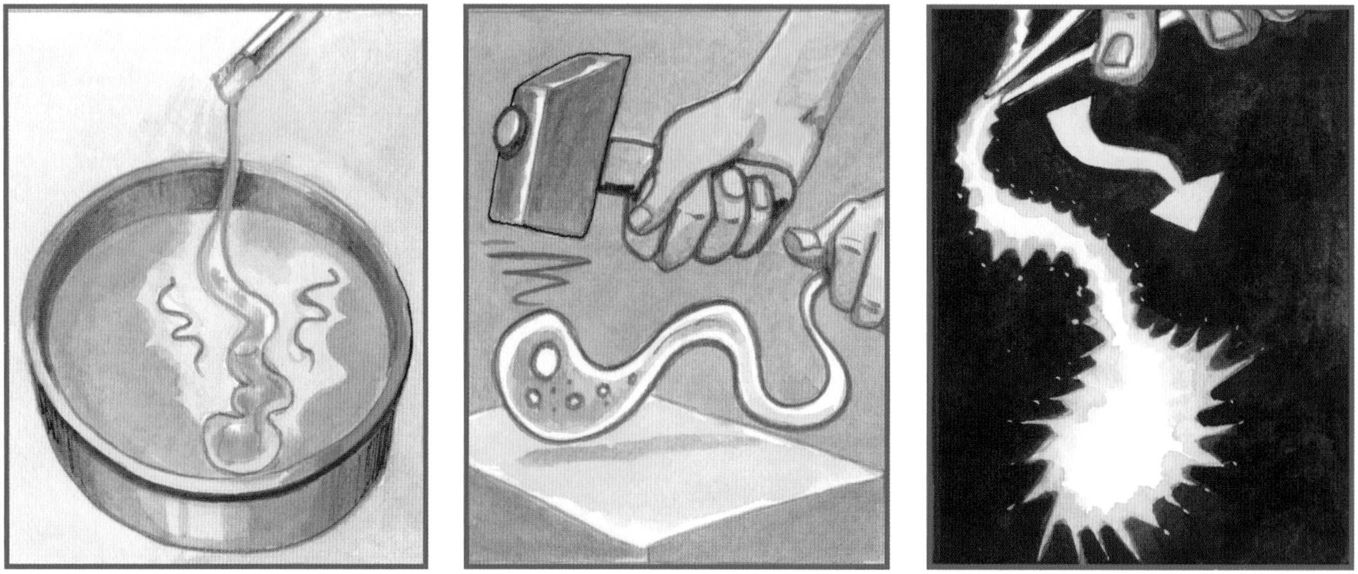

Did you know?

The raw materials for making glass have to be heated to nearly 1,700°C (about 3,100°F) to melt them so that they mix and fuse together to form glass.

A large glassmaking furnace makes more than 440 tons of glass a day. That's enough to make around one million bottles.

'Clear' glass actually has a natural green tint because of the minerals it contains, but you can't usually see the green colour unless the glass is very thick.

When glass breaks, cracks travel through it at up to about 5,000 kph (3,000 mph). That's about four times the speed of sound.

Thanks to new manufacturing techniques, glass containers today are about 40 percent lighter than they were 30 years ago.

The energy saved by recycling the glass in one bottle would run a computer for 25 minutes, a TV for 20 minutes, or a washing machine for 10 minutes. Saving energy means that less fuel has to be burned in furnaces and power stations, and this reduces the amount of carbon dioxide, a greenhouse gas, that is released into the atmosphere.

Recycling glass saves energy, because recycled glass melts at a lower temperature than new glass.

Glass that is recycled can be back in use again in a different form within 30 days.

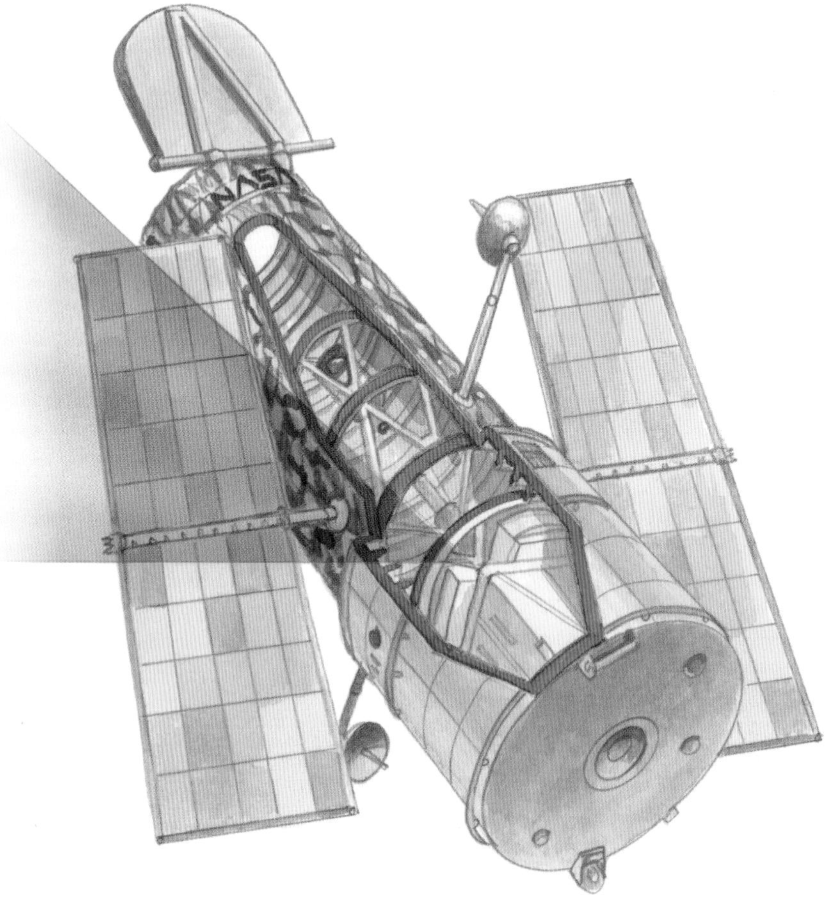